Cart used to collect the dead in the Warsaw ghetto

Foreword

The Holocaust – the attempted annihilation of European Jewry – continues to bewilder all who encounter it. Indeed it has often been described as beyond representation, so terrible was the suffering of the victims, so evil the perpetrators who carried it out.

In Britain's national museum of modern conflict, we show the efforts and sacrifice of many people, including those Allied servicemen and women who gave their lives to defeat Nazism. The Holocaust Exhibition now depicts also the nature of the evil which they helped to defeat. We have tried to relate the facts of this cataclysmic event, bringing some understanding of what happened and why. This is important for everyone, especially for young people – the Holocaust is on the National Curriculum and many schools will be visiting the Exhibition as part of their studies.

Our story centres on the destruction of the Jews, but the suffering of others whom the Nazis enslaved and murdered – Gypsies, people with physical and mental disabilities, Poles, Soviet prisoners of war, prisoners of conscience, Jehovah's Witnesses, homosexuals – is shown as well.

We begin with the aftermath of the First World War and the rise of Nazism; we end with the attempt by the SS to cover all traces of their murderous actions and the discovery of the concentration camps by the Allies. The crime which nearly sixty years ago the Nazi elite hoped would never be revealed is explained and illustrated in some detail in London for a twenty-first century audience.

To render this event in a form which stimulates interest, which conveys the horror and brutality while at the same time delivering the hard facts of history – this was the challenge we set ourselves. Film, photographs, artefacts and documents provided our raw tools of story-telling. Survivor-witnesses – people who miraculously survived the Nazi persecution and settled here after the Second World War – enriched the display with their own memories of that time. The courage and candour with which they describe their experiences provide a poignant, intimate enhancement to the main historical narrative.

We are grateful to the numerous individuals and organisations who have helped the project. A policy of annihilation leaves all too little in the way of relics, and we have been reliant on the generosity of survivors and on the cooperation of the staff and trustees of the concentration camp museums for loans and gifts of material. We are grateful also to our Advisory Group, whose understanding of the subject, guidance and support have been vital and much-appreciated throughout.

The Holocaust Exhibition documents one of the darkest chapters in the history of western civilisation. I urge you to see this exhibition and ponder its deeper meaning and the lessons it offers for the future.

Sir Robert Crawford CBE
Director-General
Imperial War Museum
June 2000

A brief history of the Holocaust

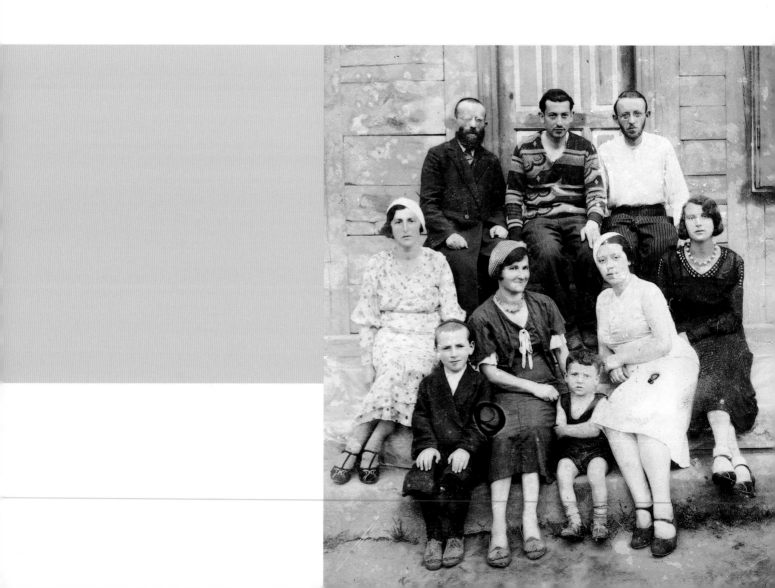

We lived like one of the Germans even though we were very Jewish at heart and at home. I had lots of friends. I was very popular. I was in the school choir and in the local sports club. I was one of them.

RUTH FOSTER

5

Europe after the First World War

The armistice of November 1918 brought peace but left Europe in turmoil. Ten million soldiers had been killed, and millions of people faced poverty and hunger. All four European empires – Germany, Austria-Hungary, Russia and Turkey – had been defeated, and new states arose out of their ruins.

In this volatile atmosphere, radical movements of the left and right flourished. The Bolsheviks had seized power in Russia and went on to suppress their rivals in a bloody civil war. Communists also briefly ruled in Hungary and the German state of Bavaria, and had tried to seize power over the whole of Germany as well. Throughout the inter-war period, Communism and the fear of Communism remained strong forces in European life.

Right-wing radicalism soon also made itself felt, often in the form of pogroms, violent attacks on Jews. Opposition groups in the former Russian Empire massacred tens of thousands of Jews in 1919-1921, and pogroms also occurred in Poland, Hungary, Slovakia and Romania.

above The Kessler family from Tomaszow Mazowiecki, Poland, all of whom perished in the Holocaust

left The Cymberknopf family from Piotrkow, Poland, before the war

My family had lived in Germany for several generations and my father in common with many Jewish people thought they were Germans first and Jewish people thereafter. We usually went to the synagogue on high holy days, but they were not a very religious family in any sense.

RUDI BAMBER

The rise of the Nazis

The Nazi party had its beginnings in a Germany suddenly defeated in war. The myth quickly spread in Germany that the army had won the war at the front but had been stabbed in the back by the 'November criminals' – communists, socialists, liberals, and businessmen who had profited from the war. As antisemites were quick to point out, they included some prominent Jews. The Versailles Peace Treaty outraged German public opinion: Germany lost territory and had to pay heavy reparations. Already under pressure from the enormous war-debt, prices began to spiral out of control, and by 1923 the German mark was worthless. Bank accounts and pension funds were wiped out, and millions of Germans were financially ruined. But debts were wiped out too, and some people made fortunes.

Against this background, the National Socialist German Workers' Party – in German, *Nazionalsocialistische Deutsche Arbeiterpartei*, NSDAP or Nazi Party for short – was formed under the leadership of Adolf Hitler. A talented public speaker, Hitler had soon recruited enough supporters, as well as a private army, the Stormtroopers (*Sturmabteilung* – SA), to try to seize power. The 'Beer-Hall Putsch' in 1923 was a failure, but it made Hitler's name.

The Nazis began to enjoy real success after the Wall Street Crash of 1929 triggered world depression, and by 1932 they had become the largest party in Germany. Hitler was appointed Chancellor at the head of a right-wing coalition on 30 January 1933. After new elections in March, Hitler had the Communist deputies arrested, and with the support of all parties except the Social Democrats he secured passage of an 'enabling law' which made him dictator.

Jewish life before the Nazis

Europe's pre-war Jewish population was concentrated in Eastern Europe, especially Poland. There the Jews had their own distinctive culture and language, and were considered a nation apart. Some of the eastern Jews and most Jews in Western Europe were fully integrated into the surrounding society, though they remained members of a religious minority. In the Mediterranean world there were many Sephardic Jews, descendants of Jews expelled from Spain in the 15th century, who still spoke a form of Spanish called Ladino.

Everywhere, Jews were adapting their traditions to the modern world. Their religion emphasised logical thought, patience and self-discipline, and these qualities proved generally useful. In Western Europe, as Jews entered the mainstream of society, many became outstandingly successful. Forced into money-lending and trade in the Middle Ages, the Jews had developed expertise in these areas. Several Jewish families such as the Rothschilds became prominent bankers, while others succeeded in various branches of business. Jews also became successful in professions such as medicine and law, and hundreds gained fame in science and the arts, sports, and many other fields. In Eastern Europe, the Jews founded their own political parties, schools and charities. They published their own newspapers and wrote novels, essays, poetry and plays — in Yiddish and Hebrew, as well as in Polish, Russian and German. A number of Yiddish-language films were made, and eastern Jews who emigrated to America made a significant contribution to the development of the Hollywood film industry.

These successes aroused anger and envy among those who believed that the Jews were aliens who should be kept in their place.

Hitler at a Nazi Party rally before coming to power

An arson attack on the *Reichstag* (parliament) in February 1933 gave Hitler an excuse to arrest thousands of
political opponents, Jews, Gypsies, and others. The first 'concentration' camps were set up to hold these prisoners.
This photograph shows a roll-call at Dachau, which served as a model for future camps.

In May 1933 Nazi students ransacked university, public and private libraries for books by Jews, Communists and others considered to be 'disruptive influences'. The students, helped by SA men, burned the books in huge public bonfires. Works by writers as diverse as Sigmund Freud, Bertolt Brecht, Jack London and H G Wells were destroyed.

Berlin policeman with an SS man, March 1933. The SS (*Schutzstaffeln* – Protection Squads) were Hitler's personal bodyguard and the elite of the Nazi private army. After the Nazis took power, the SS rapidly became the key instrument of Nazi terror and control. On Hitler's orders, the SS murdered leaders of the rival SA during the 'Night of the Long Knives' (30 June 1934), and by 1936 their leader Heinrich Himmler had taken control of the police, including the notorious Gestapo (*Geheime Staatspolizei* – Secret State Police).

The longest hatred

The hatred of Jews which the Nazis exploited had its roots in centuries of contempt and persecution. As the only religious minority allowed to exist in Christian Europe, the Jews had at various times been massacred, expelled, marked out with special signs or clothing, or forced to live in squalid walled-off districts called ghettos. Medieval attitudes gradually changed, and by 1918 Jews had gained full civil rights in most countries. But many people still resented equal rights for Jews, and as religious prejudice faded new reasons for hating the Jews were found.

Christians had traditionally believed that the Jews were cursed because of their refusal to accept Christianity. Their sufferings and inferior position in society – in reality the result of Christian persecution – were explained as God's punishment. When restrictions against the Jews were lifted, and the Jews not only proved the equal of Christians but out-competed them in many areas, those who clung to the old beliefs could only think that the Jews had achieved their successes through guile and deceit. In the 19th century the belief took root that Jewish success was the result of a powerful international conspiracy. Thus the Jews came to be the only group to be simultaneously despised as inferior and accused of being powerful and sinister.

At the same time the authority of religion was being replaced by that of science, and Jew-haters began to look for a 'scientific' justification for their beliefs. They found it in the notion of race. According to the theories of a Frenchman, Comte Joseph de Gobineau, and an Englishman, Houston Stewart Chamberlain, Europe was locked in a struggle between the 'Aryan' and 'Semitic' races, with the future of civilisation hanging in the balance. Opposition to the 'Semitic race' – the Jews – was thus made into a seemingly respectable theory, called antisemitism.

Unlike religious Jew-haters, the new 'antisemites' no longer wanted to convert the Jews, since conversion could not change a person's race: they began to think of more drastic solutions to what they called the 'Jewish question', which they regarded as a central problem for the future of mankind.

The racial state

The ideas of race and racial struggle were central to Nazi ideology. Although the Nazis regarded all 'non-Aryans' as inferior, they viewed the Jews in particular as dangerous enemies. They blamed the Jews for wars, revolutions, plagues and economic crises, and they ascribed all competing ideologies, such as Christianity, liberalism, socialism, communism and capitalism, to 'Jewish influence'. They believed that the German people, descended from noble 'Aryan' warriors, had been softened and corrupted by this influence, and that getting rid of the Jews would make Germany strong again. They regarded this as their most important mission.

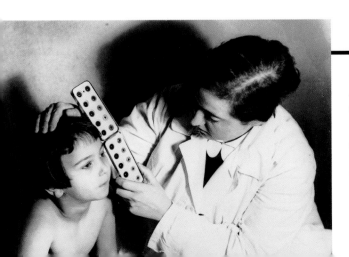

above Instruments used by Nazi 'race scientists' to examine eye and hair colour and measure skull dimensions

left The Nazis were keen 'race scientists'. Teams of researchers classified human groups throughout Germany, measuring skull shapes, eye and hair colour, body types, height and bone structure. Their aim was to record the 'racial' composition of the German population and to identify influences considered harmful.

This particular teacher, who was the headmistress of the school, brought in big cardboard pictures of Jews. They called them 'Stürmer Jews', with big noses, flat feet, big bellies, bushy eyebrows. And they said: 'These are the Jews. These are the vermin of society. They have to be destroyed.' And one girl got up and said: 'But Ruth Heilbronn – that was my maiden name – doesn't look like that. Neither do her parents nor the other Jewish people in this town.' So she punished her. She got lines to write and was sent out of the class.

RUTH FOSTER

Not only Jews were the victims of the new racism: the Nazis applied racial ideas to other groups who have traditionally been targets of bigotry. Blacks, 'Gypsies' (members of certain tribes with nomadic traditions, mainly the Roma and Sinti), and other groups came to be regarded as 'racially' inferior and undesirable. Finally, similar thinking began to be applied to people with disabilities and others regarded as deviant, such as homosexuals, 'asocials', and the mentally ill.

Such ideas – called 'eugenics' or 'racial hygiene' – were very popular in the early years of the 20th century, and not just in Germany. For example most American states had laws against mixed-race marriages, and in Sweden the mentally ill could be sterilised against their will.

When the Nazis took power they founded 33 university-affiliated or independent research institutes to study 'racial hygiene'. They also promoted the 'Aryan' ideal through films, posters and other propaganda, and offered German women incentives to have children. But those whom the Nazis considered racially inferior were discouraged or prohibited from having children. People alleged to have hereditary physical or mental disabilities were often sterilised.

Outcasts

Once in power, the Nazis began to pass laws to isolate the Jews: Jews were expelled from the army, the civil service, professional associations, and sports and social clubs. Throughout Germany signs were put up forbidding Jews to enter inns, restaurants, parks, and even entire villages. Jews, and 'Aryans' who associated with them, were often humiliated in public. Anti-Jewish and racial propaganda was ceaselessly driven home, through rallies, radio broadcasts, newspapers, films, books, posters, in schools, and by means of travelling exhibitions. The Nazis censored and then gained control of all the media, so that no opposing voices could be heard.

In 1935 the Nazis introduced the Nuremberg Laws, which stripped the Jews of citizenship, defined them by 'racial' criteria, prohibited mixed marriages and made sex between Jews and non-Jews a serious crime called *Rassenschande* ('race defilement'). Under the Nuremberg Laws, anyone with at least three Jewish grandparents was considered a full Jew, while people with one or two Jewish grandparents were considered *'Mischlinge'* of the first degree (half-Jews) or the second degree (quarter-Jews).

The 35,000 Jewish war veterans who had won medals for bravery during the First World War had until then been exempt from the worst of the anti-Jewish laws, but now even they began to suffer.

above In 1937 the 'Reich Centre for Fighting the Gypsy Menace' defined the supposed 'racial characteristics' of Gypsies. 'Flying task groups' combed Germany trying to register, photograph, and fingerprint all Gypsies. From 1938 large numbers of German Gypsies began to be imprisoned in concentration camps.

right Vienna, March 1938: Jews are forced to scrub the pavement while their neighbours look on. The *Anschluss* was accompanied by scenes of brutality towards Jews which had not been seen even in Germany.

The Nazi threat

Although the Nazis introduced a barrage of racial laws, there was relatively little physical violence at first. An initial outbreak of physical assaults on Jews by the SA (Stormtroopers) was soon stopped, and the SA itself was purged in June 1934. The Nazis had promised law and order, and since they were not yet securely in power they still had some concern about public opinion.

The Nazis were especially anxious to make a good impression for the XIth Olympic Games, held in Berlin in 1936. Reluctantly, they let competitors of all 'races' participate. Visible evidence of racial discrimination was concealed. Antisemitic signs were temporarily removed and violence was suppressed. Berlin's Gypsies were forcibly moved to a temporary camp at Marzahn on the city's outskirts, where visitors would not see them. With recovery from the Great Depression under way, Germany appeared prosperous, clean and peaceful. Many foreign visitors left Germany that year impressed by the supposed achievements of the Third Reich.

The propaganda success of the Olympics was followed by a series of successes in foreign policy. While Britain and France pursued a policy of 'appeasement' – giving in to Hitler's demands in the hope that he would become satisfied – Hitler made one aggressive move after another. In 1936 he re-occupied the Rhineland, demilitarised since 1919. Though this move violated the Treaty of Versailles, it met with little foreign reaction. In March 1938 Germany annexed Austria with the support of many Austrians: this was called the *Anschluss* or Union. In September, under the Munich Agreement with Britain and France, he took over the Sudetenland, the predominantly German-speaking western part of Czechoslovakia. These moves were accompanied by a great increase in arms production as Germany prepared for war.

In the meantime thousands of Jews were trying to emigrate from Nazi Germany, even though it meant leaving most of their property and assets behind. Concern over the increasing flow of refugees prompted the US to organise an international conference on refugees, which met in the French spa town of Evian in July 1938. Only the Dominican Republic and the international enclave of Shanghai proved willing to loosen their restrictions. Fear of stimulating antisemitism and fear that immigrants would 'take our jobs' were cited.

Kristallnacht

The successes of 1938 made the Nazis more confident and less concerned about public opinion. After the nations had shown at Evian that they were reluctant to take Jews in, the Nazis decided that more pressure needed to be applied. They were prepared to use drastic means.

On the night of 9–10 November 1938 a wave of organised violence against the Jews broke out across Germany and Austria, with Hitler's approval. More than 7,500 Jewish shops were wrecked, leaving the streets littered with glass. This gave the pogrom its name, *Kristallnacht* – the Night of Broken Glass. Nearly half the synagogues in Germany were burned down and the rest were damaged. While police stood by, Stormtroopers in civilian clothes broke into Jewish homes, terrorising and beating men, women and children. Ninety-one Jews were murdered and over 20,000 men were arrested and imprisoned in concentration camps. Afterwards the Jewish community was fined one billion Reichsmarks to pay for the damage which the Nazis themselves had caused.

After *Kristallnacht*, Jewish businesses were expropriated, private employers were urged to sack Jewish employees and offices were set up to speed emigration. Imprisoned Jews could buy freedom if they promised to leave the country, abandoning their assets.

Kristallnacht provoked outrage abroad and helped swing public opinion against appeasement. In March 1939 Hitler induced Slovakia to declare independence and then – violating the Munich agreement – occupied most of the rest of Czechoslovakia. In the same month he took over the Lithuanian port of Memel. With the public now feeling strongly that Hitler had to be stopped, Britain and France issued a guarantee to Poland, Hitler's obvious next target: if Germany invaded, Britain and France would go to war.

Thousands seek refuge

As war approached, the number of Jews emigrating from Nazi Germany increased dramatically. Britain responded by agreeing to take in Jewish children, provided that they would not be a burden on the state. Desperate parents flooded Jewish organisations in Germany with applications. Private organisations in Britain, particularly the Refugee Children's Movement, arranged travel – the so-called *Kindertransports* – and accommodation. Eventually 9,354 children arrived in Britain under the *Kindertransport* scheme, the last train leaving Berlin on 31 August 1939, the very eve of war. Most of the children never saw their parents again.

Britain also controlled immigration to Palestine, the ancient Jewish homeland, to which many thousands of Jews clamoured to go. In 1917 Britain had pledged to establish a 'national home' for the Jewish people in Palestine, a promise resented by Arab nationalists. Britain gained control of Palestine after the First World War, but Arab unrest led Britain to place strict limits on Jewish immigration with the 1939 White Paper. At a time when hundreds of thousands of Jews were trying to leave German-controlled areas, Jewish immigration to Palestine was to be limited to 75,000 over the next five years. Although the Nazis' murderous actions could not have been foreseen at this stage, the effect was that Jews were barred from their 'national home' at a crucial time.

By the outbreak of war about half of Germany's 500,000 Jews had left the country, along with 125,000 from Austria and 20,000 from the newly-acquired Czech lands.

left *Kindertransport* arrivals in Harwich

above left Torah scroll from Kolin, Czechoslovakia, burnt by the Nazis. The destruction of synagogues and religious artefacts continued after *Kristallnacht*, especially in Austria and German-occupied areas of Czechoslovakia.

far left Jewish-owned shop on the Potsdamer Strasse in Berlin, damaged during *Kristallnacht*

'Euthanasia'

The Second World War broke out on 1 September 1939 when Germany invaded Poland. A few weeks later, the Nazis launched the first of their large-scale killing programmes, code-named 'programme T4', under which 70,000 people alleged to be mentally and physically disabled would be murdered by gas, starvation, and lethal injections. The programme was personally authorised by Hitler.

T4 officials assessed patients in all German hospitals and asylums. Those considered 'unworthy of life' (*lebensunwert*) were sent to six centres where doctors killed them with carbon monoxide gas, pumped into sealed rooms disguised as shower installations. The bodies were burned in crematoria in the basements.

Relatives and people living near killing centres soon suspected the truth. In 1941 some churchmen and jurists protested, but the programme had already reached its target. Hitler officially halted T4, but similar programmes continued, aimed at concentration camp prisoners, foreign workers considered 'useless' and disabled Poles and Germans.

A separate children's programme, authorised before the war, was developed systematically after 1941. It killed more than 5,000 children and young people. In all, 170,000 people died in the various 'euthanasia' programmes.

above The staff of the Hadamar mental home in 1942. Though the T4 assessors and killing-centre staff were selected from among Nazi sympathisers, ordinary doctors in hospitals all over Germany submitted patients for assessment. Very few refused to take part.

right Manfred Bernhardt, photographed here with his sister Gerda, was a victim of the T4 'euthanasia' programme

One day the German soldiers got hold of a couple of very orthodox Jews who had this black silky coat – a kaftan – and they had earlocks and beards. And they shouted to the tenants to throw down scissors. And I was amazed at how many windows opened and how many pairs of scissors were thrown down by our Polish neighbours. And then they viciously attacked their beards and side-locks. I do remember they were actually getting hair and pulling it out. I just couldn't understand – we were children – why were they so cruel?

ESTHER BRUNSTEIN

Terror strikes Poland

Germany attacked Poland on three sides with massive forces. Then on 17 September the Soviet Union joined the attack, under a secret protocol of the recently-signed Molotov-Ribbentrop agreement. The last Polish units surrendered on 5 October and Poland was divided between the victors.

In their half of Poland, the Nazis established the 'General Government', ruled by Dr Hans Frank, while areas to the north and west were incorporated into the German Reich.

Poland was the territory that the Nazis coveted as *Lebensraum* ('living space'). They aimed to erase all vestiges of Polish nationhood, to settle the annexed areas with ethnic Germans ('*Volksdeutsche*'), and to turn the General Government into a pool of slave labour working for the German Reich. To achieve these aims, the Nazis ruled occupied Poland by terror. About 1,800,000 non-Jewish Polish citizens were killed as a result.

In Soviet-occupied Poland mass deportations of Polish citizens began. In 1939-1940 over one million people were transported in primitive cattle wagons to labour camps in Arctic Russia, Siberia and Kazakhstan. Among them were some 200,000 Jews, most of whom had fled from the German to the Soviet occupation zone in 1939.

The nearly two million Polish Jews who had now come under Nazi control were singled out for special

measures. All Jews over the age of twelve had to wear a white armband with a blue Star of David; in the annexed territories they had to sew yellow stars onto their clothing. Communities were ordered to create Jewish Councils, which were made to carry out German orders under threat of death. Jews were subject to arbitrary violence and many were forced to work in labour camps under appalling conditions. Some 100,000 died during this period of 'minor terror' (1939-1940).

In 1940 the Nazis forced most of the Polish Jews into ghettos, many of them walled- or fenced-off areas in which Jews were effectively imprisoned. By mid-1941 all the larger Jewish communities in German-occupied Poland had been sealed off.

left Hersz Izrael Laskowski and his father, Rabbi Eliasz Laskowski, were humiliated and then hanged with eight other Jews in the town of Warta

next page A young girl weeps over the body of her sister, killed by German bombs in September 1939. During the invasion of Poland over 50,000 civilians were killed.

Hitler conquers Europe

After the fall of Poland came several months of peace, called the 'phoney war'. Then Germany invaded Denmark and Norway in April 1940, and Belgium, the Netherlands and France in May. When France capitulated in June, Hitler was the master of Europe from Poland to the Pyrenees. Italy, Germany's ally, had in the meantime taken Albania and was fighting in Greece. In April 1941, German and Hungarian troops invaded the Balkans, and within a month Germany and her allies controlled that region as well.

News reaches Britain, 1939—1940

After France fell in June 1940, Britain was the only power still at war with Germany. Most occupied countries established Governments-in-Exile in London, maintaining contact with their homelands by couriers and radio. Information reached Britain through these governments and from many other sources. Britain also monitored German radio communications, and managed to break important German codes. Through these channels, Britain was reasonably well-informed of events in occupied Europe.

Invasion of the Soviet Union

On 22 June 1941 Germany broke its treaty with the Soviet Union and invaded in overwhelming force. With this invasion, Nazi fanaticism reached new levels and terror turned into systematic mass murder.

Code-named Operation Barbarossa, the invasion was Hitler's crusade against 'Jewish Bolshevism'. The Soviet leadership was caught unprepared and the German army reached the outskirts of Moscow by December. Three million Soviet prisoners of war were taken in the first eight months. Jews and suspected Communists among them were shot immediately; the rest were mostly left to starve or freeze to death in makeshift camps. Behind the front lines, SS murder squads known as *Einsatzgruppen* ('Action Groups') began rounding up and shooting Jews and Communists. Jews not killed by these squads were packed into newly-created ghettos similar to those in occupied Poland.

Mass grave, Proskurov, Ukraine. The four *Einsatzgruppen* were helped by local collaborators as well as German police and army personnel, totalling at least 30,000 people. In the south, Romanian army units also took part. Between 1941 and 1944, these mobile killing units murdered over two million people, the great majority of them Jews.

It was up to the children — youngsters like me — to obtain food. And the only way was to go down onto the sewers and over onto the Aryan side. I got caught many times, and very often I was handed over to a patrol, beaten up and thrown back into the ghetto. My father realised that I had grown up overnight and I was pretty well the breadwinner in the family.

KITTY HART-MOXON

Ghettos

The ghettos in which Jews were forced to live were overcrowded, often walled slums, which no-one could leave or enter without a special permit. There was little food, money or work, and conditions became increasingly desperate. Some 500,000 Jews died in ghettos from starvation or disease.

In March 1942, 'resettlement' of the Jews to unknown destinations began.

Rumours soon spread about the true destination of those taken away. Though the Nazis used various ruses to counter these rumours, the Jews gradually became convinced that those being 'resettled' were being taken to their deaths.

People tried to save themselves and their families in various ways. They built secret 'bunkers' in which to hide during round-ups, tried to escape from the ghettos and find hiding places on the 'Aryan side', or tried to get work in factories and workshops producing goods for the German war effort. Young political activists began to make plans for armed resistance. But most people were too hungry, ill or demoralised to resist.

above left The Jews had to cross this bridge across an 'Aryan' street to get from one section of the Warsaw ghetto to the other. The Warsaw ghetto, with 490,000 Jews, was the largest of all. Despite the ghetto's isolation, a lively smuggling trade grew up which supplemented official rations of less than 300 kilocalories daily.

above right The ghettos suffered from poor sanitary conditions and overcrowding; for example the Warsaw ghetto held 30% of the city's population in just 2.4% of its space, an average of three people per room. This helped typhus, tuberculosis and other diseases to spread.

Hundreds and hundreds of people would die daily. And they were buried in mass graves. But a lot of people couldn't afford even a mass burial or any burial. And they would throw the bodies on the streets at night — covered in paper or uncovered. And carts would come later on in the morning when the curfew stopped to collect those dead bodies. So it was a horror of us children of stepping on someone or seeing it.

EDYTA KLEIN-SMITH

top Jews boarding a 'resettlement' train. The Jewish Councils which administered the ghettos were forced to co-operate in these round-ups and faced agonising dilemmas. As it became clear that 'resettlement' meant death, they had to decide whether it was better to co-operate in the hope that some could be saved, or to take a principled stand and risk reprisals. The leader of the Warsaw ghetto, Adam Czerniakow, committed suicide rather than comply, but 'resettlement' went ahead anyway.

above Despite all efforts to keep the ghettos alive through smuggling or work, many people still died. It became common to see dying and dead people lying in the streets. 78,000 people died of disease and starvation in the Warsaw ghetto alone.

'Resettlement'

As the Jews learned too late, 'resettlement' meant being murdered in specially-built death camps.

The idea of building these camps developed by stages. Mass killing was at first done by shooting, but this was deemed inefficient. To improve on it the SS borrowed personnel, equipment, and techniques from the T4 'euthanasia' programme, which had been stopped after killing more than 70,000 people.

The latest 'euthanasia' technique was the gas van. Victims were ordered into these vans, after which the doors were locked and the motor was run, pumping exhaust fumes into the back. In 10-15 minutes, when the victims were dead, the van was driven to a secluded place and the bodies were buried in mass graves.

The gas vans were effective but limited. It became clear that if millions of people were to be murdered, purpose-built installations like the 'euthanasia' centres would be needed, but on a vastly increased, industrial scale.

The first of these death factories opened in December 1941 at Chelmno, near Lodz. It was built at the request of local Reich Governor Arthur Greiser, who wanted to 'cleanse' his area of Jews. At Chelmno, gas vans were used to kill about 150,000 Jews, mostly from Lodz and the surrounding area, and several thousand Gypsies. Three more camps opened in the spring of 1942 near the villages of Belzec, Sobibor and Treblinka in occupied Poland. Their main purpose was to exterminate the Jews of the General Government, a project code-named *Aktion Reinhard*. Instead of gas vans, the *Aktion Reinhard* camps used gas chambers fed by exhaust fumes from stationary diesel engines. They were capable of killing thousands of people at a time. As in the 'euthanasia' programme, the gas chambers were disguised as showers to deflect suspicion.

Aktion Reinhard was stopped in the autumn of 1943 and all traces of the camps were destroyed. 1,600,000 Jews and thousands of Gypsies had been murdered in them.

top Personal belongings of Jews, excavated from the site of the Chelmno death camp

left SS-*Sturmbannführer* (Captain, later Major) Christian Wirth, commandant of Treblinka and then Belzec death camps. Later inspector of the *Action Reinhard* camps.

Jewish armed resistance

The Nazi programme to exterminate the Jews of Eastern Europe did not go unopposed. Revolts broke out at Treblinka, Sobibor, Auschwitz and in more than 40 different ghettos, mostly in eastern Poland. Revolts in the camps hastened their closure. Elsewhere, especially in Belarus and Lithuania, Jews escaping from the ghettos took up arms as partisans, either independently or with Soviet or other partisan groups. In all, 30,000 Jewish partisans fought the Nazis in Eastern Europe.

The best-known example of Jewish armed resistance was the Warsaw Ghetto Uprising. During the main deportations from the Warsaw ghetto in the summer of 1942, Jewish youth groups formed the Jewish Combat Organisation (JCO). A few pistols were smuggled into the ghetto, and shots were fired at police during a second, three-day deportation *Aktion* in January 1943. More weapons were obtained, enough to arm a few hundred fighters. When the Nazis resumed clearing the ghetto on 19 April they were met by organised fighting groups of the JCO, led by 23-year-old Mordechai Anielewicz, and the Jewish Military Union. The rest of the ghetto's inhabitants disappeared into a maze of underground bunkers.

To force people out of the bunkers, the Nazis burned down the ghetto, building by building. The JCO's command bunker fell on 8 May, but isolated fighting groups continued to hold out. On 16 May Jürgen Stroop, the German commander, ordered Warsaw's main synagogue to be blown up to mark the end of the revolt. He reported that 7,000 Jews had been killed in the fighting. The 45,000 Jews who survived the Warsaw Ghetto Uprising were deported to labour camps and the Majdanek concentration camp. All Jews in these camps were shot on 3–4 November 1943, in what the Nazis cynically called the *Erntefestaktion* ('Harvest Festival action').

Jews offered armed resistance to the Nazis elsewhere. More than a million Jews fought in the Allied armed forces. Jews fought with Tito's partisans in Yugoslavia and participated in the French Resistance, in both mainstream and separate Jewish units. The main French group called itself *L'Organisation Juive de Combat*, in honour of the Warsaw fighters.

News reaches Britain, 1941–1943

Since British Signals Intelligence could decode radio messages from some of the mobile killing units, the Government knew about large-scale massacres in the East virtually as they happened. In a speech on 24 August 1941, two months after the Nazi invasion of the Soviet Union, Churchill acknowledged that mass murder was going on, calling it 'a crime without a name'. He had been informed that the victims were almost all Jewish civilians, but spoke instead of 'Russian patriots defending their native soil'.

Reports transmitted by the Polish Government-in-Exile and through neutral Switzerland gradually made the picture clear over the summer of 1942. In June a report from the Jewish Workers' Bund in Poland reached London, stating that 700,000 Jews had already been killed. On 8 August Dr Gerhart Riegner, the World Jewish Congress representative in Switzerland, notified Jewish leaders in the US and Britain that a plan was 'under consideration' to exterminate all the Jews in Nazi-occupied territory 'at one blow'. Though inaccurate in some details, Riegner's telegram was based on information from a well-placed source within Nazi Germany and was the first report of a systematic extermination plan to reach the West. But Riegner passed it on 'with all due reservation' and a British official dismissed it as 'a rather wild story'. In November 1942 Polish courier Jan Karski came to Britain with detailed messages about the destruction of the Polish Jews. He met Foreign Secretary Anthony Eden, then travelled to the US where he saw President Roosevelt.

The outcome of these developments was that on 17 December the Allies issued a joint declaration condemning the Nazi extermination policy and threatened the perpetrators with punishment after the war. The declaration was read to the House of Commons, which stood for a minute's silence. It was broadcast several times over the BBC and 1.2 million leaflets denouncing Nazi war crimes were dropped on German cities during air-raids early in 1943. These propaganda efforts had little effect.

Pressure mounted on the US and British governments to do something more substantial to aid the Jews. This included statements by the Archbishops of Canterbury, York and Wales and by MPs such Eleanor Rathbone urging that more be done to help Jewish refugees from Nazi Europe. On 19 April 1943, the day that the Warsaw Ghetto Uprising broke out, British and American officials met in Bermuda to discuss the refugee problem. As at Evian five years earlier, little was decided. Not until January 1944, when five million Jews were already dead, would there be any substantial initiatives.

Survivors of the the Warsaw Ghetto Uprising are led through the
burning ghetto to waiting deportation trains

The 'Final Solution'

While the outside world and the Jews themselves struggled to understand what was happening in occupied Europe, the Nazis were refining and working out their plans. The initial mass killings of Jews do not seem to have been part of an overall plan of total extermination, since not all Jews were killed and new ghettos were created. Official Nazi policy until October 1941 was to get rid of the Jews through emigration, though under wartime conditions this was increasingly unrealistic. Ghettos were created as a temporary measure, and several plans for a Jewish reservation were considered.

The idea of the total extermination of Jews – what the Nazis called 'the Final Solution of the Jewish question in Europe' – seems to have developed late in 1941 and was put into effect from the spring and summer of 1942. The Nazi state was a maze of competing agencies, which were expected to show initiative. It is likely that the Final Solution was not the result of a single order, but unfolded with Hitler's approval as officials following his ideas to their logical conclusion out-did each other to impress their superiors. Hitler had threatened in January 1939 that a new world war would mean 'the annihilation of the Jewish race in Europe': Nazi officials gradually worked out how best to implement this threat.

The Final Solution involved an enormous array of organisations – not only the SS, German State administration and police forces but also the army and private industry. Private companies supplied crematory ovens, gas vans and poison gas. The army lent the killing squads equipment and personnel, and carried out its own killings. Various branches of the state administration organised deportation trains, decided on timetables and priorities, processed the victims' possessions, and cajoled foreign governments into rounding up Jews to be killed.

above and right In most countries they controlled, the Nazis ordered Jews to sew a yellow star onto their clothing. Anyone caught without one could be imprisoned or shot. Reminiscent of the marking of Jews in the middle ages, the yellow star was first introduced in the annexed areas of Poland in 1939, and in other countries from 1941. The star was meant to humiliate the Jews and mark them out for segregation and discrimination. Later it made them easy to round up and deport.

far right In countries across Europe Jews were rounded up and packed into ghettos or transit camps, usually near railway lines. Victims to be 'resettled' were then crammed into cattle wagons, up to one hundred people in each. The journeys lasted days, in freezing cold or stifling heat, often without food, water, or toilet facilities. Many of the deportees died before reaching their final destination.

The atmosphere was an atmosphere of despair. Babies were crying, couples were fighting with each other, arguments. And the fear which everybody had, the unknown of what's going to happen to us.

FREDDIE KNOLLER

27

Deportation: the rest of Europe

The measures used to prepare and carry out the Final Solution varied from country to country, but in general were more barbaric in Eastern Europe and the Balkans than in the West. The Jews were also worse off where the Nazis were directly in control than in countries where independent governments had to be pressed to hand Jews over. Such countries varied in their attitude: Vichy France, for example, willingly surrendered Jewish immigrants but balked when it came to native French Jews. Slovakia, headed by a Catholic priest, allowed Jews to be deported but exempted those who had converted to Christianity. Finland handed over seven immigrants with criminal records but otherwise refused to co-operate. Croatia and Romania carried out their own anti-Jewish and anti-Gypsy programmes, massacring large numbers. Bulgaria surrendered 11,000 Jews from areas of Greece it had occupied, but protected Bulgarian Jews.

In countries where the Nazis were in direct control, anti-Jewish measures were ordered by German governors or *Reichskommissars*. In countries that remained independent, the orders came from local governments such as the Vichy regime in France, with varying degrees of pressure from the German Foreign Office. Everywhere, round-ups and deportations were carried out by local police and officials, often helped by collaborationist movements such as the Rexists in Belgium or the Dutch National Socialist Movement.

Some Jews managed to escape or delay their fate by living under assumed names or hiding. In the Netherlands one in six went into hiding. Parents often tried to save their children by placing them in non-Jewish homes, Catholic orphanages, or other institutions.

We stepped outside. We just didn't know where we were. There were all kinds of things happening. There were people in striped uniforms, shaven heads. It looked like an actual madhouse. So we looked at each other and we said, 'but surely this is not meant for us. We will be sent somewhere else. This is not for people, not for us.' And the people who were working there, we asked them, 'Where are we? Where are we?' And they said, 'You don't know where you are? You're in Auschwitz.' 'And what is Auschwitz? What's Auschwitz?' 'Well, you come here, but very few go out of here.' And they actually pointed to sort of smoke belching, chimneys. And said, 'That's what happens to people. That's what happens.'

ESTHER BRUNSTEIN

Selection at Auschwitz II-Birkenau, from a set of photographs taken by an official SS photographer during the Hungarian *Aktion* in 1944 and mounted in an album which was discovered after the war. They are the only surviving photographs of the selection process in a death camp.

Women and children were separated from the men and they were sitting in a small wood which was just across from our barracks. Children would pick flowers, the women would sit and picnic and give children some food and drink which they brought with them. And they were led into Crematorium Four . . .
Now the people in the woods were totally calm. They had no idea that the people that had gone in in front of them were already dead.

KITTY HART-MOXON

Jewish women running to the gas chambers, from the only known set of photographs taken at Auschwitz by prisoners. Members of the *Sonderkommando* (prisoner work crew) at Crematorium V took these pictures using a camera stolen from the SS.

Auschwitz-Birkenau

The great majority of those deported from across Europe were brought to Auschwitz. Situated at the geographical centre of the Nazi empire in the industrial region of Silesia, Auschwitz was the biggest of the death camps and the last to go into full-scale operation. It was where the Nazis perfected their killing technology.

A huge complex of 39 camps and sub-camps, Auschwitz was not only an extermination centre but also the largest component of the Nazi slave-labour system. Between 1940 and 1945 about 400,000 prisoners suffered starvation and terror in the Auschwitz camps. The prisoners included 205,000 Jews, 140,000 Christian Poles, 25,700 Gypsies and 17,000 Soviet citizens (mostly prisoners of war). The thousands of prisoners of other nationalities included a few British prisoners of war.

Non-Jews were assigned to the labour camps, but Jews were subjected to 'selection' on arrival: about one-fifth of the 1.1 million Jews brought to the camp were selected for work, while the rest went to the gas chambers.

A million Jews, 70,000 Christian Poles, 23,000 Gypsies, 15,000 Soviet prisoners and thousands of others died in the Auschwitz labour camps or were murdered in its gas chambers, which included such refinements as electric lifts to carry the bodies up to the crematoria.

The mortuary of the original crematorium at Auschwitz I, the original camp, was used as a gas chamber late in 1941 and again for several months late in 1942. For murder on a larger scale, two abandoned farm houses at the much bigger camp at Birkenau (Auschwitz II), were converted into gas chambers in the spring of 1942. These could kill several hundred people at a time, and were in use for a year. The bodies were buried in nearby pits, but were later dug up and burned.

Four purpose-built complexes, called Crematoria II, III, IV and V, were completed between March and June 1943. Each consisted of an undressing room, a gas chamber capable of killing 2,000 people at a time, and a set of crematory ovens which worked day and night to burn the bodies. At peak times bodies were also burned in open pits. The ovens were supplied by the firm Topf and Sons of Erfurt, and various other German firms contributed gas-tight doors and other equipment.

A staff of more than 7,000 – officers, doctors, administrators and guards – served in the Auschwitz complex. These men and women came from many backgrounds. They included locksmiths, an accountant, a baker, a carpenter, a musical instrument maker, a bank clerk, a fireman, dentists and farm labourers.

Although those who requested transfer to other duties were regarded as weak, and their careers might be impaired, no one was forced to participate in the murder process. Those who did take part were motivated by their belief in Nazi ideology, a misplaced desire to 'do a good job', or to avoid being sent to the front, and sadism or blood-lust.

Can of Zyklon B. A commercial pesticide, Zyklon B was originally used to kill vermin. The Nazis first used it to kill human beings in August 1941 when 20–30 Soviet prisoners of war were murdered in an improvised gas chamber at Auschwitz I. Five to seven kilogrammes of the pellets produced enough hydrogen cyanide gas to kill 1,500 people.

A number was tattooed on our arm and we were told that from
now on I am only 157103.

FREDDIE KNOLLER

33

The concentration camp system

The Auschwitz complex was the largest of an immense system of concentration camps spread throughout Europe.

From four original camps in Germany (Dachau, Buchenwald, Ravensbrück for women and children and Oranienburg, later called Sachsenhausen), the system grew into thousands of different camps and sub-camps organised into 23 major complexes, holding about two million prisoners. In addition some 4,500,000 Soviet POWs were held in makeshift camps, often nothing more than open-air enclosures where prisoners were left to starve or freeze to death.

There were many different kinds of camps, created for different purposes. Among them were concentration camps (*Konzentrazionslager*, abbreviated KZ or KL), labour camps (*Arbeitslager*), transit camps (*Durchgangslager*), 're-education camps' and so on. At most camps, prisoners were subjected to hard labour, starvation, and harsh punishments, and the death rate was very high. Apart from the original four, the most notorious concentration camps included Mauthausen, Natzweiler, Mittelbau-Dora, Stutthof, Gross Rosen and Bergen-Belsen.

Vernichtungslager (extermination camps) existed only to kill people, 98% of them Jews. The four *Vernichtungslager* were Chelmno, Belzec, Sobibor and Treblinka.

Auschwitz and Majdanek served as both extermination and concentration camps. There were also two smaller camps, Maly Trostinets in Belarus and Semlin in Serbia, where extermination operations took place using gas vans.

top Clubs from Breendonk camp, Belgium. Many such instruments were custom-made by the SS and *Kapos* for their personal use.

above Eating-bowl of Czech prisoner Prem Dobias. To lose one's eating bowl could be fatal as they were very hard to replace. Prem added nettles to his watery soup to provide some essential vitamins.

left Auschwitz registration photos. Newly-arrived prisoners at Auschwitz had their numbers tattooed onto their left forearms to help the guards identify them, alive or dead.

left Slave labourers at Fort Breendonk camp in Belgium.

right Some prisoners could bear their torment in the camps no longer and committed suicide, either by running onto the electrified barbed wire fence or by hanging themselves in a barrack hut.

The whole camp was counted. It all had to tie up. If one was missing, the whole hell could
break out. One day, unfortunately, one Greek girl was so ill she didn't march into the camp.
Nobody spotted her. The whole camp has been standing for three hours or more, and in the
end when they found her they dragged her into the camp and they set dogs on her. And this
is how she died. And that was the day I spat into the face of my God.

MARIA OSSOWSKI

Inside the camps

More than two million men, women and children toiled in the vast Nazi camp system. They were of all nationalities,
races, faiths and ideologies deemed enemies by the Nazis. Nearly half were murdered, or died as a result of the
appalling conditions.

Everything was done to dehumanise prisoners and rob them of their individuality. On arrival, their
possessions were confiscated, their heads shaved, and their clothes replaced by ill-fitting and often filthy uniforms.
They were identified not by their names but by numbers, which at Auschwitz were tattooed onto their forearms. They
also wore identifying patches, usually triangular, sewn onto their uniforms: red for 'political' prisoners, green for
'professional criminals', yellow for Jews, and so on. This made it easy to single them out for special treatment. Some
categories of prisoners, such as 'professional criminals', were put in authority over other prisoners or given preferred
jobs. Others, particularly Jews, homosexuals, Poles, Gypsies and Soviet prisoners of war, were treated especially
harshly.

Prisoners faced overcrowded barracks in which epidemics of typhus and dysentery raged. They slept
sardine-fashion on wooden bunks for four hours a night, then had to stand outside for hours in all weather for roll-
call. They worked long hours for starvation rations and were whipped if they could not keep up the pace. Punishments
included heavy and pointless labour, flogging with a thick cane, hanging and various forms of torture.

SS doctors routinely performed medical experiments which killed their 'patients' or left them hideously
deformed. Prisoners who were sick or injured could report to the camp hospital, tended by other prisoners with
medical knowledge, but few medicines and little equipment were available. The SS frequently carried out 'selections'
in the camp hospitals, using lethal injections to kill prisoners judged unable to work or sending them to be gassed.

Unable to cope with these conditions, many prisoners committed suicide or became *Muselmänner*
('Muslims') – camp slang for fatalistic prisoners who had lost the will to live, and who rarely survived for long.

Resistance by prisoners was difficult but did take place. In addition to the revolts at Treblinka and Sobibor,
Jews who worked in the crematoria at Auschwitz revolted in October 1944, setting fire to Crematorium IV. Other
resistance movements within the camps were usually organised by Communist prisoners or the Polish underground.
Members first helped each other survive, then infiltrated the camp administration. Once in positions of authority,
they were able to help others, often saving hundreds of lives. By the end of the war, some camps were almost
entirely in the hands of these red-badged 'politicals'.

News reaches Britain, 1943–1944

Late in 1943 and in the spring of 1944 several prisoners escaped from Auschwitz and later wrote reports on the killing facilities. These reports reached Geneva, and were sent to Britain in June.

News about mass deportations to Auschwitz from Hungary prompted calls to bomb the camp or its railway approaches. Britain and the US rejected these proposals as impracticable, though industrial targets in the Auschwitz area were bombed. Allied governments generally responded to calls for action by saying that the best way to save lives was to win the war as soon as possible. But for the Jews, who faced complete annihilation, the end of the war would come too late.

Action on a limited scale was finally taken in 1944, more than a year after the Allied Declaration had officially acknowledged that an extermination campaign was under way. In January, the US established the War Refugee Board (WRB) to aid relief and rescue. The WRB helped send Swedish diplomat Raoul Wallenberg to Budapest to aid the remaining Hungarian Jews, and sent relief supplies to occupied Europe.

Rescue and survival

To a limited degree, it was possible for Jews to leave Nazi-dominated Europe during the war. Legal emigration from some parts of Nazi-occupied territory was still possible until October 1941, and tens of thousands of Jews made their way illegally to Switzerland, Spain, Sweden and Turkey. The Nazis also offered to exchange Jews for money or goods.

Some Jews living in pro-German states were saved when their governments either refused to co-operate with the Nazis, or stopped deportations after a time. Most Italian Jews and nearly all the Jews of Bulgaria and Finland survived in this way, along with some in Hungary and Slovakia.

right This *Schutzpass* (protective pass) saved the life of Mrs Imre Pataki. It was issued by the Swedish diplomat Raoul Wallenberg, who was funded by the US War Refugee Board.

far right Henri Obstfeld

Story book sent to Henri Obstfeld while in hiding by his parents. Henri's parents, who were also in hiding, did not see their son for nearly four years. They were reunited with him only after the war, by which time Henri was five.

Businessmen and other well-connected people occasionally used their influence to protect Jews. Diplomats were especially well placed to rescue people by issuing visas and other documents.

It is estimated that about 200,000 Jews survived in hiding, or by pretending to be 'Aryans' with the help of false identity documents. Both Jews and their protectors feared betrayal, and were hunted by blackmailers and the police. Penalties for helping Jews were severe: more than 1,000 people lost their lives, and many more were sent to concentration camps. One third of the Jews in hiding died.

Between 1941 and 1945, Paul Sondhoff was hidden in a small cupboard by his elderly piano teacher in Vienna – a space so cramped that he later developed deformities. One of his few possessions during that time was this small clockwork bear.

Destroying the evidence

As the Nazis retreated, they tried to hide all evidence of their crimes. They erased all traces of the *Aktion Reinhard* camps. 'Special Commandos' of prisoners, under SS *Standartenführer* (Colonel) Paul Blobel, dug up and burned the remains of hundreds of thousands of victims before they themselves were killed. Early in 1945 the Nazis blew up the crematoria at Auschwitz-Birkenau and began to transport or force-march surviving prisoners of the camps deep into Germany.

above 'They chased us all into a large barn. Since we were five or six thousand people, the wall of the barn collapsed from the pressure of the mass of people and many of us fled. The Germans poured out petrol and set the barn on fire. Several thousand people were burned alive. Those of us who managed to escape lay down in the nearby wood and heard the heart-rending screams of the victims.'

Menachem Weinryb, an escapee from the Gardelegen death march, April 1945

top Prisoners on a death march from Dachau. As the Allies advanced, hundreds of thousands of prisoners were force-marched from camp to camp. Starving and weak, poorly clothed and with no proper shoes, the prisoners walked for weeks through snow and rain, sleeping in barns or in the open. Tens of thousands died from cold or hunger, or were shot for not keeping up.

above Bone-grinder used by the Blobel Commandos. After the bodies had been burned and sifted for valuables, large bones were crushed in a bone-grinder and then scattered over nearby fields as fertiliser.

above right A survivor kisses the hand of a British soldier at Bergen-Belsen

When I came back to the barrack and told my sister that we were free, my sister
didn't know any more. And she passed away eight days after the liberation.

TAUBA BIBER

41

Discovery

In the closing months of the war in Europe, forward units of the Allied armies advancing from east and west came across the concentration camps.

Horrified at what they saw, the liberators forced German soldiers and civilians to view the camps, and sometimes to help bury the dead. Newspapers, radio broadcasts and newsreels spread the news throughout the world.

Although the existence of the concentration camps was well known, until they were liberated few people fully understood what they were like. The news coverage which they now received shocked and horrified public opinion everywhere. In Britain Bergen-Belsen, liberated by British troops, came to symbolise Nazi atrocities. It was also where most of the Jews still alive in the camp system were concentrated, making up two-thirds of the camp's inmates; but few people noticed this fact or commented on it.

Relief efforts could not stop more victims from dying of malnutrition or in the epidemics which swept the camps. The rehabilitation and repatriation of survivors continued long after the war in Europe ended on 8 May 1945.

War crimes trials

Only a fraction of the tens of thousands of people directly involved in carrying out the Holocaust were identified and put on trial after the war. A few committed suicide before they could be tried. Others escaped justice by assuming false identities or moving abroad. Most were simply not prosecuted.

In August 1945, 23 nations signed an agreement on the punishment of major war criminals. Allied tribunals and German courts tried senior Nazis, concentration camp officials, *Einsatzgruppen* members, Nazi doctors and other professionals. Many others were extradited to the countries where they had committed their crimes. Some 5,000 lower-ranking Nazi personnel were convicted over the next four years.

A few of those convicted were executed. Those given prison terms were often released early, particularly if their skills made them useful to the opposing powers in the Cold War. The process of bringing Nazi war criminals and their collaborators to justice has continued into the twenty-first century.

The Nuremberg trial defendants in court. The International Military Tribunal held at Nuremberg in 1945, which tried the top surviving Nazis, was the best-known of hundreds of war crimes trials carried out immediately after the war. The great majority of those involved were never tried, however.

Supported by the
Heritage Lottery Fund

left Detail from a model featured in the Exhibition. It depicts the selection of 2,000 Hungarian Jews from the Berehevo ghetto at the Auschwitz II-Birkenau death camp in May 1944.

Published by the Imperial War Museum,
Lambeth Road, London SE1 6HZ

© The Trustees of the Imperial War Museum 2000

Reprinted in 2000, 2002, 2004, 2006, 2008

ISBN 1 901623-24-6

Inside the camps

Arrival

The procedures used on arrival at a concentration camp were meant to dehumanise and terrorise. Prisoners had their possessions confiscated, and were classified, photographed, numbered, shaved of all body hair and deloused. They were sometimes left standing naked in freezing weather or subjected to other indignities. They were issued with ill-fitting clogs and striped uniforms that were often filthy with water or faeces. The uniforms had coloured patches to denote the category of prisoner.

Prisoners not selected for immediate death were made to work, usually at hard physical labour with long hours, brutal treatment, and starvation rations. German firms could buy the labour of these slaves from the SS.

More than two million men, women and children toiled in the vast system of labour and concentration camps. They were of all nationalities, races, faiths and ideologies deemed enemies by the Nazis. Nearly half were murdered, or died as a result of the appalling conditions.

E CRUDE
DEFENCE.
HUMAN
GROUND.
SURVIVOR